COC

and

ESSENTIAL OILS

for

DOGS

Dogs Health Care Using Safe Natural Remedies

JAMIE CLAY

DEDICATION

For Snowy and Terri.

CONTENTS

Disclaimer

This document is geared towards providing exact and reliable information in regards to the topic and issue covered. The publication is sold on the idea that the publisher is not required to render an accounting, officially permitted, or otherwise, qualified services. If advice is necessary, legal or professional, a practiced individual in the profession should be ordered.

From a Declaration of Principles which was accepted and approved equally by a Committee of the American Bar Associate and a Committee of Publishers and Associations.

The information provided herein is stated to be truthful and consistent, in that any liability, in terms of inattention or otherwise, by any usage or abuse of any policies, processes, or directions contained within is the solitary and utter responsibility of the recipient reader. Under no circumstances will any legal responsibility or blame be held against the publisher for any reparation, damages, or monetary loss due to the information herein, either directly or indirectly.

The information herein is offered for informational purposes solely and is universal as so. The presentation of the information is without a contract or any type of guarantee assurance.

The trademarks that are used are without any consent, and the publication of the trademark is without permission or backing by the trademark owner. All trademarks and brands within this book are for clarifying purposes only and are the owned by the owners themselves, not affiliated with this document..

INTRODUCTION

First of all, I would like to thank and congratulate you for downloading this book ***Coconut and Essential Oils for Dogs: Dogs Health Care Using Safe Natural Remedies.***

This book provides you a how-to guide to treating and care various dog health problems using safe natural remedies complete with recipes.

Chapter 1 starts out by talking about health benefits of Coconut Oils, how to use Coconut Oil and Basic guide in giving Coconut Oil to your dog with useful tips.

Chapter 2 provides you some useful Coconut Oil recipes for caring your dog, i.e. Coconut Oil anti-itch cream, antibiotic cream, immune booster, and paw balm.

Chapter 3 starts talking about Essential Oils for dogs with a list of safe and unsafe Essential Oils used in the recipes. List of safe Essential Oils is accompanied by their properties and beneficial features.

Chapter 4 guides you on how to source and select Essential Oils. What you should consider, look for, check and be careful of when sourcing and selecting Essential Oils.

Chapter 5 provides you guide on blending, handling, and storing Essential Oils. What factors to consider when blending Essential Oils, What should you do and avoid when handling Essential Oils, Things to keep in mind when storing Essential Oils.

Chapter 6 guides you how to apply Essential Oils on your dog. There are five steps you need to follow to get the best result in applying Essential Oils on your dog. You will also find methods of application.

Chapter 7 as the highlight of this book provides you with Essential Oils recipes for various dog health problems, i. e. Eliminating bad odor, helping with skin problems, flea and tick repellent, mosquito repellent, ear care, wound care, anxiety, arthritis, calming dog hyperactivity, motion sickness, upset stomach, and sinus infections relief.

This book provides you with all the information you need to know about Coconut and Essential Oils and safe application on your dog. By using Essential and Coconut Oils you can provide safe and natural remedies for your dog's various health problems.

Thank you again and enjoy!

CHAPTER 1 – BENEFITS OF COCONUT OIL FOR DOGS

Coconut Oil is one of the most stable oils in treating your dog's health problems. It is a liquid substance that's derived from the matured flesh of a palm tree coconut.

Coconut oil is a rich source of protein and has great health benefits. It has 90% saturated fats; most of the fats are Medium Chain Triglycerides (MCT). The main component of MCT is Lauric Acid.

Lauric Acid which makes up 50% of the oil provides antifungal, antiviral, anti-microbial and anti-bacterial properties. It helps to fight common dog infections and improve the health of your dog.

HEALTH BENEFITS OF COCONUT OIL FOR DOGS:

1. Helps Relieve And Clear Up Skin Conditions such As:
    a. Itchiness
    b. Flea Allergies
    c. Prevents and Treats Yeast and Fungal Infections
    d. Eczema
    e. Contact Dermatitis
2. Prevents Dry Skin
3. Moisturizes Paw Pads
4. Moisturizes Cracked Nose
5. Gives Your Dog a Beautiful, Healthy Coat

6. Disinfects Cuts
7. Promotes Wound Healing and Great For Bites And Stings
8. Improves Better Digestion
    a. Improves Digestion and Helps The Body To Absorb Vitamins And Nutrients
    b. Treats Bad Breath and Even Eliminates It
    c. Helps To Heal Digestive Disorders Such As Colitis And Inflammation.
9. Improves Bone Health
10. Enhances Metabolic Function
11. Enhances Immune System
    a. Increases Energy and Helps Reduce Weight
    b. Helps to Prevent Or Control Diabetes
    c. Promotes Normal Thyroid Function
    d. Helps with Arthritis
12. Improves Dog Breath and Oral Health
    a. Improves Bad Breath
    b. Whitens Teeth
    c. Prevents Plaque
    d. Heals Gums
13. Cleans Your Dogs Ears

14. Uses To Reduce Odor Especially In Aging Pets Without Excessively Bathing Your Pet.

HOW TO USE COCONUT OIL:

1. Internally – As a Food Supplement

When you supplement your dog's diet with Coconut Oil, remember to start slow. Bear in mind that giving your dog too much coconut oil hastily can result in digestive and detox problems.

Large amounts of this component can cause diarrhea so begin with small amounts and just increase gradually.

Slowly increase the amount after a few days and no problem has occurred. Once your dog appears to be uncomfortable, lethargic, or has diarrhea, just reduce the amount temporarily.

Coconut oil is best given with solid or liquid food at any meal.

Basic Guide In Giving Coconut Oil As Food Supplement:

- First few days
    - ¼ teaspoon daily for puppies or small breeds
    - 1 teaspoon daily for large breeds.
- After that
    - 1 teaspoon for every ten pounds of body weight daily.
    - 1 tablespoon for every thirty pounds of body weight daily.

2. Externally - As a Topical Treatment For Skin Issues

As a topical treatment for skin issues just rub a generous amount of coconut oil directly onto your dog's skin and dog's infections such as minor bites, foot pads, and sores.

Try to keep your dog engaged for some time after the application for it is slow absorbing.

USEFUL TIPS

- It is recommended that you only use extra-virgin organic Coconut Oil on your dog.
- Of course, with any supplements, a dog's intake should be monitored and it's best to consult your vet when it comes to any health issues with your dog.

CHAPTER 2 - COCONUT OIL RECIPES FOR DOGS

COCONUT OIL ANTI-ITCH CREAM

Ingredients:

- 8 oz. Extra-Virgin Organic Coconut Oil
- 10 drops Lavender Essential Oil
- 2 drops Lemon Essential Oil

Tools:

- 1 small glass bottle

Directions:

---

1. Put the Coconut Oil in a small glass bottle.
2. Let it melt in the room temperature.
3. Add the essential oils.
4. Shake or stir to mix well.
5. Topically massage your dog's skin once a week (or more often it needed).

COCONUT OIL ANTIBIOTIC CREAM

Ingredients:

- 4 tbsp. Coconut Oil
- 12 drops Oregano Essential Oil

Directions:

1. Put the Coconut Oil in a glass jar or bottle
2. Let it melt in the room temperature.
3. Add the essential oils.
4. Mix with a spoon
5. Topically massage your dog's skin

COCONUT OIL - TURMERIC IMMUNE BOOSTER

Ingredients:

- 1/4 cup Extra-Virgin Organic Coconut Oil
- 1 cup filtered water
- 1/2 cup Organic Turmeric Powder
- 1 1/2 Black Pepper, freshly ground

Directions:

1. Place the coconut oil in a saucepan with the filtered water.
2. Heat the mixture on low heat - until it melts.
3. Add the Turmeric Powder and the Black Pepper.
4. Stir all the ingredients over low heat about 10 minutes or until it forms a thick paste.
5. Let it cool
6. Place it in a jar with a lid

7. Store the paste in your refrigerator for up to two weeks.
8. Give it to your dog internally as a food supplement

COCONUT OIL PAW-BALM

Ingredients:

- 8 tbsp. Natural Beeswax
- 4 tbsp. Extra-Virgin Organic Coconut Oil
- 4 tbsp. Olive Essential Oil
- 2 tbsp. Shea Butter

Tools:

- 1 small pot
- 2 glass storage jars or tins

Directions:

1. Put all the ingredients in a small pot over a low heat.
2. Stir until melted and well blended.
3. Pour the mixture into storage jars or tins.
4. Let it cool and hardened.

5. Cap and label the balm for external use.

Tips

- It is better using storage containers with a wide mouth so you can easily glide your dog's paw across the surface to apply.
- Keep the balm away from direct heat.

CHAPTER 3 – ESSENTIAL OILS FOR DOGS

Naturally plants survive by implementing some self-defense mechanisms such as:

1. Producing scents to attract insects or animal to aid their reproductive processes.
2. Producing oils to deter enemies, either insects, animals or other plants that may eat or harm them.

Those scents and oils, which are produced by plant cells in and around specialized glands, are then extracted/distilled (most frequently by steam or water) into a high concentrated liquid known as essential oils.

Almost every part of plant glands ranging from flower, petals, peels, berries, leaves, stems, bark, wood or roots can be utilized.

A usual essential oil contains more than 100 different chemical compounds, each of which shows a specific therapeutic property, and for this cause, many essential oils can be used for such a large range of situation.

Properties found in almost all essential oils include:

- **Antiseptic properties**
- **Antifungal properties**
- **Antiviral properties**
- **Antibacterial properties**

Essential Oils have shown many health benefits for both human and your pets, especially your dogs. Dogs react really well to essential oils and when used safely can be used for supporting the physical wellness of your dog to the emotional well-being.

Benefits of using Essential Oils for your dogs are as follow:

- Help to prevent and eliminate bad odor (see Bad Odor Elimination Recipe)
- Help your dog with his/her skin problem (see

Skin Problem Recipe)

- Help your dog with itching problem (see Anti-Itch Recipe)
- Help to repel flea and tick (see Flea and Tick Repellent Recipe)
- Help to repel mosquito (see Mosquito Repellent Recipe)
- Help to care your dog's ear (see Ear Care Blending Spray Recipe)
- Help your dog recovering from wound (see Wound Care Recipe)
- Help your dog with anxiety (see Anxiety Relief Recipe)
- Help to relieve your dog's arthritis (see Arthritis Relief Recipe)
- Help to calm your dog hyperactivity (see Dog Hyperactivity Spray Recipe)
- Help your dog from suffering motion sickness (see Motion Sickness Spray Recipe)
- Help your dog from suffering upset stomach (see Upset Stomach Recipe)
- Help to relieve sinus infection of your dog (see

Sinus Infection Relief Recipe)

LIST OF SAFE ESSENTIAL OILS (USED IN THE RECIPES)

Bergamot

- Anti-fungal with soothing effects.
- The perfect remedy for ear infections resulting from yeast or bacterial overgrowth.
- Due to its propensity to cause photosensitization, due caution should be taken when using this oil by keeping the dog away from the sun after use.

Carrot Seed

- Contains anti-inflammatory properties.
- It is also tonic and has moderate anti-bacterial effects.

- Good for improving the immunity of dog skin by fighting dehydration, flakiness as well as skin sensitivity.
- Rejuvenate and stimulate tissue generation, making it effective for scar healing.

Cedarwood

- Contains antiseptic, tonic and circulation-stimulating properties.
- Repelling fleas.
- Skin conditioning properties and may, therefore, be used to fight dermatitis of all types.

Chamomile, German

- The German Chamomile is an anti-inflammatory, non-toxin, gentle and safe oil that may be used to deal with skin conditions, allergic reactions, and burns.

Chamomile, Roman

- Roman Chamomile is an analgesic, nerve-calming and antispasmodic oil that is good for soothing the central nervous system and is also effective for soothing muscle pains, teething pains, and cramps.

Citronella

- Contains anti-fungal properties that help to treat insect bites.
- Can help treat and prevent colds, fevers, and calm barking dogs

Clary Sage

- Good for calming and sedating the nerves (when used in small diluted amounts)

Eucalyptus Radiata

- Contain anti-viral properties.
- It is also an expectorant, contains anti-inflammatory properties that therefore makes it suitable for relieving chest congestion and repelling fleas.

Frankincense

- Helps build and maintain a healthy immune system, promote cellular health, calming and soothing to the skin.
- Promote your dog's body natural healing process.

Geranium

- Contains anti-fungal properties.
- Help fight fungal infections in the dog's ears
- Good for skin irritations
- Assists in repelling ticks.

Ginger

- Aids digestion
- Effective for treatment of motion sickness.
- Effective for relieving pain caused by certain infections such as arthritis, sprains, dysplasia, and strains.

Helichrysum

- Contains anti-inflammatory, analgesic as well as regenerative effects.
- Highly therapeutic.
- Excellent for skin conditions and irritations such as eczema.
- Effective for healing of bruises, scars and pain relieving.

Lavender

- Contains anti-bacterial, anti-itch and nerve-calming properties.

- Perfect fit for a wide range of common dog ailments such as skin irritations and allergic reactions.

Marjoram, Sweet

- Strong anti-bacterial and soothing properties.
- Perfect fit for muscle relaxation.
- Good for wound care.
- Insect repelling.
- Fighting infections caused by bacteria.

Myrrh

- Contains powerful antimicrobial, astringent, expectorant, antifungal, stimulant, carminative, stomachic, anti-catarrhal, diaphoretic, vulnerary, antiseptic, immune booster, circulatory, tonic, anti-inflammatory and antispasmodic.

Niaouli

- Contains powerful anti-bacterial properties.
- Though it is highly antihistaminic, it is less likely to cause skin irritations in the dogs.
- The perfect remedy for ear infections and general skin conditions caused by allergies.

Orange, Sweet

- Calming, deodorizing and flea-repelling essential oil.
- Like Bergamot, this oil can also cause photosensitization, hence, should be used in cool areas away from the sun.

Peppermint

- Stimulates blood circulation and is also an insect repellent.
- Relieve from muscle spasms.
- Treat motion sickness in the dog (combine with Ginger).

Ravensara

- Strong antiseptic, antibacterial and antiviral properties.
- Effective to treat numerous infectious skin conditions.

Rose Geranium

- Contains antiseptic properties.
- Effective aid to help with burns, wounds, ulcers and other skin problems.

Rosemary

- Help reduce nervous tension and fatigue.
- Soothes muscle aches and pain.
- Support healthy digestion.

Sunflower

- Boost energy.
- Strengthen the immune system.
- Improve skin health.
- Prevent cancer
- Reduce inflammation.

Valerian

- Effective for calming the nerves in the dog.
- Perfect for treating dog anxiety that may result from such incidences as noise or ever separation.

Vetiver

- Supports healthy circulation, calming, grounding effect on emotions, immune-enhancing properties.
- Contains antiseptic properties that help gently cleanse the skin.

Ylang Ylang

- Provides relief from stress, anger, and anxiety.
- Prevents wound from infections and speeds up the healing process.
- Helps maintain healthy skin.

LIST OF UNSAFE ESSENTIAL OILS

The following essential oils are considered hazardous due to the fact that they cause skin irritations, allergic reactions and may lead to a wide spectrum of infections to your dog. The following are some of these oils; Anise, Birch, Bitter, Hyssop, Juniper, Thyme [Red or White], Pennyroyal, Rue, Cassia, Camphor, Horseradish, Goosefoot, Garlic, Cloves, Sassafras, Savory, **Tea Tree Oil**, Tansy, Wormwood, Yarrow, Wintergreen, Terebinth.

CHAPTER 4 – SOURCING AND SELECTING ESSENTIAL OILS GUIDE

As we started to apply essential oils to our pet, we need to learn some basic steps in order to get the best results.

We will discuss these basic steps in the following sections. First, we will learn how to source and select the best essential oils for our furry friends.

When sourcing and selecting essential oils for your dogs the followings need to be put into your consideration:

Look Out For Certain By-Words

First, always look out for certain by-words and catch-phrase such as:

- Fragrance Oil
- Nature Identical Oils
- Perfume Oil

As they may indicate an essential oil is not pure, hence not safe for your dog.

Be Careful Where You Buy the Oils

Secondly, only buy from selected and reputed outlets, as opposed to supermarkets and health food stores, as these are known to sell cheaper but low-quality essential oils.

Things you should ask yourself when researching an essential oils supplier are:

- The reputation of the company.
- Whether the supplier has its own distillers or has relation with one.
- Track record, expertise, and good governance practice of the supplier.

Be Careful Of False Promotions

Check certain promotional terms such as:

- Aromatherapy Grade
- Therapeutic Grade

Spend On Quality

Always spend on quality essential oils although they are a bit pricey. It is important that you avoid suspiciously cheap oils, as these may be adulterated.

Check the Packaging

Quality essential oils are often bottled in amber, cobalt or violet glass bottles. Avoid any oils sold in any other bottles other than these or in plastic bottles.

Check the Product Information Provided

Lastly, check for provided product information of the oils. This kind of information is normally printed on the label or may be available on the store's website or brochure. When looking out for this kind of information, always ensure there are:

- The Scientific Name of the Oil As Well As Its Common Name.
- Method Of Extraction,
- Country Of Origin, Method Of Cultivation (Whether Organic, Cultivated or Wild Harvested)
- The Phrase '100% Pure Essential Oil'.

CHAPTER 5 - BLENDING, HANDLING, AND STORING ESSENTIAL OILS GUIDE

The following are some of the factors to consider when blending essential oils for dogs:

- **The Chemistry of the Oil**
- **The Desired Action**
- **The Sequence of the Blend**

Other than the three basic factors above, there are some general rules to follow when blending essential oils. They are:

- Lighter and smaller molecules normally produce thinner oils that are more volatile while heavier and larger molecules produce thicker oils that are less volatile.
- Lighter and smaller molecules absorb faster in the dog's body while heavier and bigger molecules absorb slower.
- All in all, after creating your preferred blend, let it sit for a few days before you decide how effective it is. This is often an ample time for the constituents within the oils to get cozy with each other.

HANDLING ESSENTIAL OILS GUIDE

Some tips for handling essential oils are as follow:

Never Over-Expose

- Never over-expose your dog to the blends as they might develop toxicity due to overuse.

Do Not Spill into the Dog's Eyes or Ear Canal

- When handling these oils, always ensure the oils do not spill into the dog's eyes or ear canal as this may cause undue aversions to the oil.

Always Avoid Applying the Oils to the Dog's Paws

- When applying essential oils, keep in mind to always avoid applying the oils to the dog's paws, as these are where the dog sweat glands are located.

STORING ESSENTIAL OILS GUIDE

Storing your essential oils is just as important as their application, and you should follow carefully the steps given here to maintain the integrity of the oil.

Bear in mind the following in storing the Essential Oils:

- It should be stored in a cool and dry place away from direct heat or light
- Keep it away from children and your dogs.
- Leave some air space in the bottle so that the oil can breathe.
- Don’t use plastic bottles.

- Don't forget to label each bottle with the name, date of purchase and shelf life

CHAPTER 6 - APPLYING ESSENTIAL OILS TO DOGS GUIDE

As essential oils contain more than 100 different chemical compounds, each of which exhibits a specific therapeutic property, these oils can help our pets fight a wide range of conditions.

This chapter will focus on the various steps to follow when applying essential oils to your dogs. The steps have been clustered as follows:

1. CHECK YOUR DOG'S SENSITIVITY

Dilute the Oil

Diluting essential oils is necessary because the chemicals contained in these oils may be stronger than the dog's skin can handle (if used in concentrated form).

Another benefit of diluting essential oil is to ensure that your dog's skin can safely absorb the oils without the irritation that would otherwise lead to aversions to the oils.

Use in Moderation

After that, the diluted blend should be applied to the dog skin in moderation. Applying the oil in moderation also ensures that some of it do not spill into undesired parts such as the dog ears or eyes.

Check Your Dog's Response

Always check your dog's response, whether he/she likes the blends or not. This step is necessary because different dogs will respond in different ways to different essential oil blends.

The response may also be influenced by your method of application. It is recommended to use common sense and good judgment to detect any lapses in the application procedure and respond to them accordingly.

Learn What Oils to Avoid

As you start using essential oils you will learn some common knowledge such as most dog skins do not respond favorably to oils that contain high phenol, such as Oregano and Thyme.

Always ensure you keep these oils away from your dog, as their usage may only pose health risks to the dog's skin instead of causing the intended healing effects.

2. MATCH THE DOSAGE WITH THE SIZE OF YOUR DOG

The next step is to apply the essential oil that match your dog's size.

- For smaller dogs, use 3-5 drops of the oil in one round of application. The oil should also be diluted 80 to 90% prior to application.
- For larger dogs, start with 3-4 drops, and dilution is not necessary unless otherwise indicated on the product label.

3. TEST YOUR DOG'S RESPONSE BY FILLING THE AIR WITH THE SMELL OF THE OIL

Test your dog's response by filling the air with the smell of the oil, either by wearing the oils around your animals or diffusing it in their space. This step is an opportune moment to know whether your dog likes the oil or not. A calm disposition will show some interest in the oil while jittery or resistant movements will indicate aversions.

4. CHOOSE THE BEST METHOD OF APPLICATION

The method of application of dog essential oils is the most important part in determining the effectiveness of the oil as well as the entire process.

As you will see in the next section, you can apply directly to your dog's skin (topically) or aromatically or ingested internally.

5. HOW TO APPLY ESSENTIAL OIL TO YOUR DOG

Once your dog and you are ready, hold the dog in a comfortable position and start applying the essential oils.

You can do that by starting to apply in smaller portions until you have successfully applied all the areas of your dog's body. Applying carefully also ensures that a great portion of this oil is not lost in the application procedure.

METHODS OF APPLYING ESSENTIAL OILS ON YOUR DOGS

Methods of application of essential oils on your dogs are as follow:

1. Topically

- You can apply essential oils to the spine, ears, or even on the toes/pads of your dogs.
- You can apply essential oils directly to the wound pretty much anywhere on the body.
- Avoid the eyes, nose, anal and genital areas.

Ways of Applying Essential Oils Topically:

- If Applying the Essential Oils in its concentrated form, use only one to two drops. Put the oil first on your palm, rub it and then apply it on the affected area.

- If Applying the Essential Oils in diluted form, put the diluted oil in a spray bottle and apply a spritz on the affected area.
- Or put ample amount of the diluted on your palm and then rub your palm together for few seconds before applying it on the desired area. Apply it by massaging into the area in a circular motion.

2. Aromatically

- Essential Oils can be used aromatically by putting a drop of essential oil on their collar or their bed.
- You can also make a spray by adding a few essential oil drop to water and spraying your dog's fur.

Other Ways of Diffusing Essential Oils:

- Cold air diffusion
- Mist spray

- Air conditioner

3. Internally / Orally

Before you make your dogs ingest essential oils, you must understand that they must be the highest quality possible. You can either put the essential oils in an empty gel capsule or your dog's food/drink if they don't mind the flavor.

It is recommended only giving one drop when allowing a dog to ingest internally.

Ways To Apply Essential Oils Orally:

- Drop to the tongue directly and should be swallowed immediately.
- Mix with the beverage (milk or water)
- Adding to meals

Consult immediately with your vet if you find the following signs:

- Diarrhea
- Vomiting
- Lethargy
- Breathing Difficulty
- Heart Palpitations
- Drooling
- Uncoordinated Gait
- Muscle Tremors
- Redness in your dog's tongue, lips, gums, or skin
- Pawing at your dog's mouth or face

CHAPTER 7 – ESSENTIAL OILS FOR DOGS RECIPES

Essential oils have shown great benefits in treating common dog problems and improving the general health of your pet.

The following are essential oils recipes that you can use to treat illnesses and improve the overall quality of life for your dog.

The Recipes are divided as follow:

I. SKIN RECIPES

1. BAD ODOR ELIMINATION

   a. Eliminate Bad Odor Dog Shampoo

   b. Eliminate Bad Odor Dog Spray

2. SKIN PROBLEMS

   a. Skin Soothing Shampoo

   b. Skin Soothing Spray

3. ANTI-ITCH

II. DOG CARE

1. FLEA AND TICK REPELLENT

   a. Flea Repellent Shampoo

   b. Flea Repellent Spray

   c. Tick Rcpellent Spray

2. MOSQUITO REPELLENT SPRAY

3. EAR CARE BLENDING SPRAY

4. WOUND CARE

5. ANXIETY RELIEF

    a. Anxiety Essential Oil Mix

    b. Anxiety Essential Oil Powder

6. ARTHRITIS RELIEF

    a. Arthritis Massage Blend 1

    b. Arthritis Massage Blend 2

7. CALMING DOG HYPERACTIVITY SPRAY

8. MOTION SICKNESS SPRAY

9. UPSET STOMACH

10. SINUS INFECTIONS RELIEF

BAD ODOR ELIMINATION

ELIMINATE BAD ODOR SHAMPOO

Ingredients:

- 8 oz. (240 ml) of all-natural shampoo
- 8 drops Lavender Essential Oil
- 4 drops Geranium Essential Oil
- 4 drops Roman Chamomile Essential Oil
- 3 drops Sweet Marjoram Essential Oil

Directions:

- Apply Aromatically or Topically

- Mix well all the ingredients
- Use as dog shampoo

ELIMINATE BAD ODOR DOG SPRAY

Ingredients:

- One cup of distilled water
- 10 drops Lavender Essential Oil
- 6 drops Peppermint Essential Oil
- 6 drops Sweet Orange Essential Oil
- 3 drops of Eucalyptus Essential Oil

Directions:

- Apply Aromatically or Topically
- Mix well all the ingredients in a spray bottle
- Spray directly on your dog's body while covering his face and eye
- Avoid spraying on your dog's head

SKIN PROBLEM

SKIN SOOTHING SHAMPOO

Ingredients:

- 8 oz. (240 ml) of all-natural shampoo
- 7 drops Lavender Essential Oil
- 6 drops Carrot Seed Essential Oil
- 6 drops German Chamomile Essential Oil
- 5 drops Geranium Essential Oil

Directions:

- Apply Aromatically or Topically
- Mix well all the ingredients

- Use as dog shampoo

SKIN SOOTHING SPRAY

Ingredients:

- 4 oz. (120 ml) of Olive/Jojoba/Sweet Almond Carrier Oil
- 7 drops Lavender Essential Oil
- 6 drops Carrot Seed Essential Oil
- 6 drops German Chamomile Essential Oil
- 5 drops Geranium Essential Oil

Directions:

- Apply Topically
- Mix well all the ingredients
- Apply a few drops of the oil blend to your dog's skin or itchy area.

ANTI-ITCH

Ingredients:

- 5 oz. olive or jojoba oil Carrier Oil
- 2-3 drops pure vitamin E
- 4-5 drops chamomile (Roman) Essential Oil
- 4-5 drops Lavender Essential Oil
- 2-3 drops Frankincense Essential Oil (optional)

Directions:

- Apply Topically
- Mix well all the ingredients in a glass dropper bottle
- Apply 2-4 drops of the oil blend to your dog's itching area two times a day.

FLEA AND TICK REPELLENT

FLEA-REPELLENT SHAMPOO

Ingredients:

- 8 oz. (240 ml) of all-natural shampoo
- 5 ~ 7 drops Peppermint Essential Oil
- 2 ~ 5 drops Clary Sage Essential Oil
- 4 drops Citronella Essential Oil

Directions:

- Apply Aromatically or Topically
- Mix well all the ingredients

- Use as dog shampoo

FLEA-REPELLENT SPRAY

Ingredients:

- 4 oz. (120 ml) of Olive/Jojoba/Sweet Almond Carrier Oil
- 5 ~ 7 drops Peppermint Essential Oil
- 2 ~ 5 drops Clary Sage Essential Oil
- 4 drops Citronella Essential Oil

Directions:

- Apply Aromatically or Topically
- Mix well all the ingredients
- Apply a few drops of the oil blend to your dog's neck, back, chest, legs, and tail.
- Also, you can add a few drops of the oil blend to your dog's cotton collar or bandanna to make an aromatic flea collar

TICK-REPELLENT SPRAY

Ingredients:

- 4 oz. (120 ml) of Olive/Jojoba/Sweet Almond Carrier Oil
- 10 drops Lavender Essential Oil
- 8 drops Geranium Essential Oil
- 6 drops Lemon Eucalyptus Essential Oil

Directions:

- Apply topically or aromatically
- Mix well all the ingredients
- Apply a few drops of the oil blend to your dog's neck, back, chest, legs, and tail.
- Also, you can add a few drops of the oil blend to your dog's cotton collar or bandanna to make an aromatic tick collar.

MOSQUITO REPELLENT

MOSQUITO REPELLENT SPRAY

Ingredients:

- 8 ounces of Aloe Vera juice
- 10 drops Myrrh Essential Oil
- 7 drops Citronella Essential Oil
- 5 drops Lemongrass Essential Oil
- 5 drops Rose Geranium Essential Oil

Directions:

- Apply Aromatically or Topically

- Mix well all the ingredients
- Apply a few drops of the oil blend to your dog's neck, back, chest, legs, and tail.
- Also, you can add a few drops of the oil blend to your dog's cotton collar or bandanna to make an aromatic flea collar.

EAR CARE

EAR CARE BLENDING SPRAY

Ingredients:

- 4 oz. (120 ml) of Olive/Jojoba/Sweet Almond Carrier Oil
- 8 drops Lavender Essential Oil
- 6 drops Roman Chamomile Essential Oil
- 5 drops Bergamot Essential Oil
- 5 drops Niaouli Essential Oil

Directions:

- Apply Topically
- Mix the oils in a dark glass bottle

- Use a dropper to drip a few drops of the oil blend into your dog's ear canal and gently massage the outside of the ear
- Right after that, clean the ear with a cotton ball.

WOUND CARE

WOUND CARE SPRAY

Ingredients:

- 4 oz. (120 ml) of Olive/Jojoba/Sweet Almond Carrier Oil
- 10 drops Lavender Essential Oil
- 5 drops Sweet Marjoram Essential Oil
- 5 drops Niaouli Essential Oil
- 4 drops Helichrysum Essential Oil

Directions:

- Apply Topically
- Mix well all the ingredients
- Store in a dark glass bottle

- Apply a few drops of the oil blend to your dog's minor cuts, bruises, scrapes, insect bites, and other small wounds.

ANXIETY RELIEF

ANXIETY ESSENTIAL OIL MIX

Ingredients:

- 4 oz. (120 ml) of Olive/Jojoba/Sweet Almond Carrier Oil
- 6 ~ 8 drops Lavender Essential Oil
- 6 ~ 8 drops Valerian Essential Oil
- 3 ~ 4 drops Sweet Marjoram Essential Oil
- 3 ~ 4 drops Clary Sage Essential Oil

Directions:

- Apply Topically

- Rub 2 to 3 drops of the essential oil blend between your hands
- Apply it on the edge of your dog's ears, on his inner thighs, between the toes, or under his "armpits".

ANXIETY ESSENTIAL OIL POWDER

Ingredients:

- Baking soda, rice flour, or cornstarch for diluting essential oils
- 3 parts of Lavender Essential Oil
- 2 parts of Bergamot Essential Oil
- 2 parts of Clary Sage Essential Oil
- 1 parts of Ylang Ylang Essential Oil

Directions:

- Use 12 to 15 drops of this essential oil blend per cup of baking soda, or use a blend of baking soda and rice flour.
- Stir or shake to mix well.
- Apply Topically

- For car ride anxiety: sprinkle the powder on a blanket and put it inside the cage with the dog.
- For separation anxiety: sprinkle the powder on your old clothes and put it on your dog's bed.

ARTHRITIS RELIEF

ARTHRITIS MASSAGE BLEND 1

Ingredients:

- 4 oz. (120 ml) of Olive/Jojoba/Sweet Almond Carrier Oil
- 8 drops Helichrysum Essential Oil
- 7 drops Valerian Essential Oil
- 5 drops Ginger Essential Oil
- 4 drops Peppermint Essential Oil

Directions:

- Apply Topically

- Rub 2 to 3 drops of the essential oil blend between your hands
- Massage your dog's sore joint or pain
- Put a drop or two on the inside of his/her ear tips.

ARTHRITIS MASSAGE BLEND 2

Ingredients:

- 4 oz. (120 ml) of Olive/Jojoba/Sweet Almond Carrier Oil
- 6 drops Lavender Essential Oil
- 8 drops Lemon Essential Oil
- 8 drops Ginger Essential Oil

Directions:

- Apply Topically
- Rub 2 to 3 drops of the essential oil blend between your hands
- Massage your dog's sore joint or pain
- Put a drop or two on the inside of his ear tips.

CALMING DOG HYPERACTIVITY

DOG HYPERACTIVITY SPRAY

Ingredients:

- 4 oz. (120 ml) of Olive/Jojoba/Sweet Almond Carrier Oil
- 6 drops Lavender Essential Oil
- 6 drops Valerian Essential Oil
- 5 drops Roman Chamomile Essential Oil
- 4 drops Sweet Marjoram Essential Oil
- 3 drops Bergamot Essential Oil

Directions:

- Apply Aromatically or Topically
- Spray this blend on your dog's coat every day
- Avoid eyes area
- Also, you can spray this blend around doorways and on bedding to repel pests.

MOTION SICKNESS

MOTION SICKNESS SPRAY

Ingredients:

- 4 oz. (120 ml) of Olive/Jojoba/Sweet Almond Carrier Oil
- 10 drops Peppermint Essential Oil
- 14 drops Ginger Essential Oil

Directions:

- Apply Aromatically or Topically

- Apply the oil blend to the inside tip of your dog's ears, under his "armpit", and on his belly
- Avoid eyes area
- Also, you can add a few drops of the oil blend to a cotton ball and put it in front of the car air vent to circulate the scent in the car.

UPSET STOMACH

Ingredients:

- 5-6 olive or coconut oil Carrier Oil
- 2-3 drops peppermint Essential Oil

Directions:

- Apply Topically
- Mix well all the ingredients
- Apply a few drops of the oil blend to your dog's stomach

SINUS INFECTIONS RELIEF

Ingredients:

- 15 ml sweet almond oil Carrier Oil
- 5 drops Eucalyptus Essential Oil
- 5 drops Ravensare Essential Oil
- 5 drops Myrrh Essential Oil

Directions:

- Apply Topically

- Mix well all the ingredients
- Apply a few drops of the oil blend to your dog's neck and chest.

CONCLUSION

Coconut and Essential Oils have shown many health benefits for both human and your pets, especially your dogs. To gain their benefits, you need to learn how to apply these oils appropriately.

This book gives you a complete guide on how to administering Coconut and Essential Oils to your dogs.

Start now and enjoy this book.

Made in the USA
San Bernardino, CA
18 January 2017